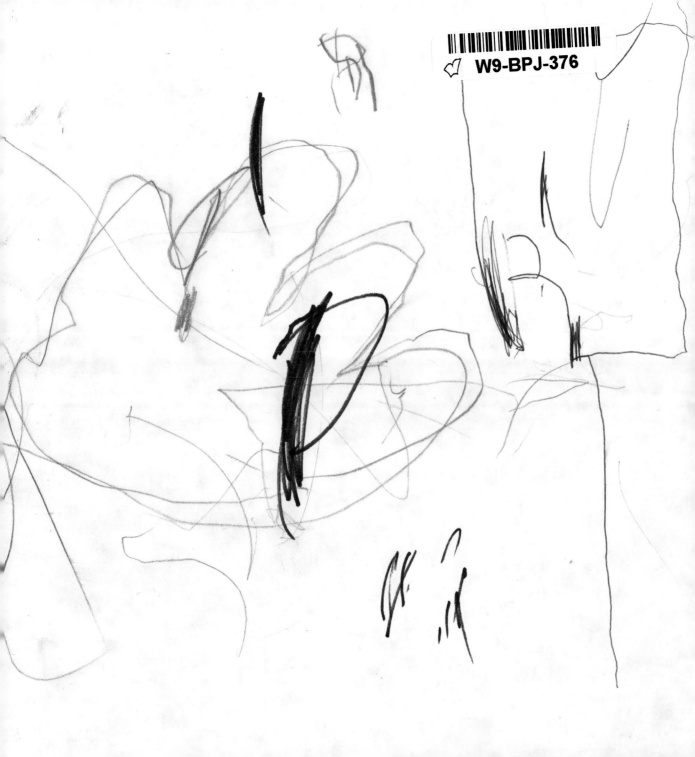

Note

Once a reader can recognize and identify the 20 words used to tell this story, he or she will be able to read successfully the entire book. These 20 words are repeated throughout the story, so that young readers will be able to easily recognize the words and understand their meaning.

The 20 words used in this book are:

cannot	fat	like	run
can't	for	not	silly
cat	good	old	that
chase	he	pair	the
dog	is	quite	too

Library of Congress Cataloging-in-Publication Data
Fehlner, Paul.
    Dog and cat / by Paul Fehlner; illustrated by
Maxie Chambliss.
       p.   cm.—(My first reader)
    Summary: Due to their obvious frailties, an old dog and a fat cat
manage to coexist relatively peacefully.
       Previously published by Grolier.
       ISBN 0-516-05353-1
       (1. Dogs—Fiction. 2. Cats—Fiction. 3. Stories in
rhyme.) I. Chambliss, Maxie, ill. II. Title. III. Series.
PZ8.3.F325Do 1990
(E)—dc20

90-30164
CIP
AC

Dog and Cat

Written by Paul Fehlner   Illustrated by Maxie Chambliss

 CHILDRENS PRESS ®

CHICAGO

Text © 1990 Nancy Hall, Inc. Illustrations © Maxie Chambliss.
All rights reserved. Published by Childrens Press®, Inc.
Printed in the United States of America. Published simultaneously in Canada.
Developed by Nancy Hall, Inc. Designed by Antler & Baldwin Design Group.

4 5 6 7 8 9 10 R 99 98 97 96 95

The dog is old.

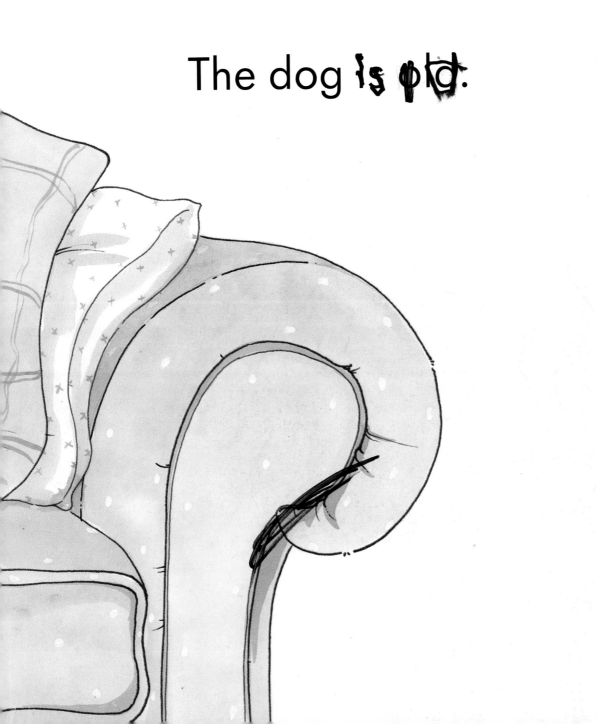

The cat is fat.

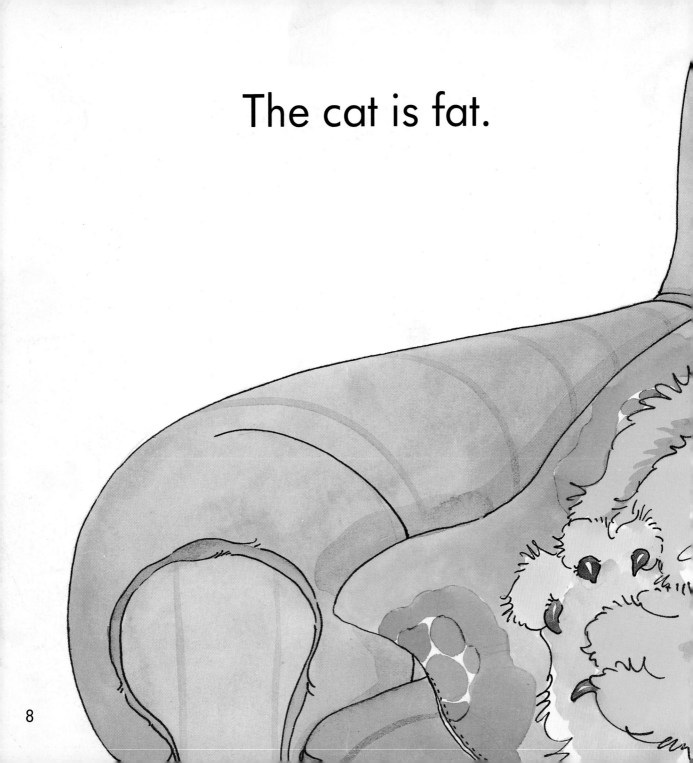

The old, old dog

can't chase the cat.

The dog is old,

not like the cat.

He cannot chase

15

the fat, fat cat.

That is quite good,

for the fat cat.

The cat can't run.

He is too fat.

That silly pair,

the dog, the cat.

The dog is old.

The cat is fat.